"There is so much yet to know, to expose and explore, to open up what we never considered, that demands our presence, to open up what we never expected and never dreamed of, to step into old and new worlds. It is a riveting adventure to follow the lines of poetry written and shared between Larry Thomas and Clarence Wolfshohl, and now with the reader. From the Great Chihuahuan Desert to the backwoods brambles of Mid-Missouri and the Central Plains they stand a 1000 miles apart under blue skies so vast, they stand together, sharing the pages of each other's lives, hearing how they reflect, recall, reinvigorate each other's lives. And to the reader, Wolfshohl writes "May your mad prophet hear the sweet soughing of my oaks."

-Walter Bargen, First Poet Laureate of Missouri
and author of *Orwell at the Kremlin*

"We're in luck that close friends Larry and Clarence have received and replied to, in intuitive ways, one another's poems. The two poets, as they write, rhythm their ways into memories—childhood, family, trees and flowers, rodeo flings, fields and forests, the evocative Texas and Missouri ecosystems of their lives lived in the mysterious meanwhile of Time as we all approach our ends. When I read two of the many portraits here, too, read them and the rest of Wolf Tree and Agave several times, Larry's "The Vaquero" and Clarence's "Tattoo Palimpsest", I realized, again, the depths of what true poetry could be, and so will you."

-William Heyen, National Book Award Finalist, author of *Nature: Selected & New Poems, 1970-2020* and *Diaspora: Fifteen Collections*

Wolf Tree and Agave

(a correspondence in poetry)

Larry D. Thomas and
Clarence J. Wolfshohl

Spartan
Press

Spartan Press

Kansas City, Missouri

spartanpresskc.com

Spartan
Press

Copyright © Larry D. Thomas and
    Clarence J. Wolfshohl 2026

First Edition: 1 3 5 7 9 10 8 6 4 2

ISBN: 979-8-89975-031-1

LCCN: 2026933016

Author photos: Lisa Thomas, Bob Elliot

Cover image: Larry D. Thomas

Title page image: Dennis Yi Adams

Acknowledgments:

Sincerest gratitude is extended to the editors of the following publications in which the poems noted were first published.

Agave Magazine: "Agave" and "Ice and Fire"
All Roads Will Lead You Home: "Fishing at Lake of the Ozarks"
Art Museums (chapbook published by Blue Horse Press): "Giant Boxes"
Borderlands: Texas Poetry Review: "Brother"
Bunchgrass Press (anthology): "As Winter Turns to Spring"
Bundle (American Amateur Press Association): "The Piscine Y"
Cenizo Journal: "Gloria" and "In All Its Array of Colors"
Civilized Beasts (anthology published by Weasel Press): "Hereford Bull," "Laden with What He Needed" and "Near Midnight"
Concho River Review: "Turkey Strut" and "Winter Nakedness"
Dragon Poet Review: "Chicory Blues"
Green Hills Literary Lantern: "Puma, Cougar, Panther, Mountain Lion" (nominated for a Pushcart Prize)
Illya's Honey: "Hands," "Spring Blooms" and "Stones"
Ink Cahoots (American Amateur Press Association): "The Bounds of Books"
Off the Coast: Maine's International Poetry Journal: "Grasses"

Pushing the Envelope: Epistolary Poems (Lamar University Literary Press anthology edited by Jonas Zdanys): "Due Cultivation" and "On Stationery of Light"

Red River Review: "Tattoo Palimpsest," "The Black-tailed Jackrabbit," "To Our Destinations," "Under the Golden Dragon" (nominated for a Pushcart Prize) and *Ursus Americanus*

Right Hand Pointing: "The Desert Heat" (nominated for a "Best of the Net" award) and "We Know We're Well"

Roundup Magazine: "Drifting to Silence" and "The Rodeo"

San Pedro River Review: "Bells," "Hooked," "Terlingua Ghost Town" and "The Ghosts of Toledo"

Southwestern American Literature: "Rough Stock" and "The Straw Hat"

The Oklahoma Review: "An Imperceptible Blip" and "The Transfer of Light"

VerseWrights: "On the Way to the Funeral," "The Sign-Painter" and "Wolf Tree"

Voices de la Luna: "Smear of Minnow-Shine," "Sotol" and "The Vaquero"

Table of Contents:

Clarence and I first met in February 1999, at the 3rd Annual Writers' Conference in Honor of Elmer Kelton (Angelo State University, San Angelo, Texas), at which each of us was a featured presenter, I of poetry and Clarence of prose. I had long been an admirer of handset letterpress books, and Clarence was one of the top handset letterpress publishers in the nation. He was the publisher of Timberline Press located in Fulton, Missouri.

Shortly after the conference, I queried Clarence as to whether he would be interested in considering one of my poetry manuscripts for publication with Timberline Press, and he graciously agreed to do so. The manuscript was titled *The Lighthouse Keeper* which was comprised of poems set entirely on Galveston Island. I had composed the poems in the summer of 1996 in a travel trailer owned by me and my wife which was permanently parked on a lot we co-owned for twelve years through our membership at the Texas Campgrounds Club located on West Beach of Galveston Island.

Approximately six weeks after I submitted my manuscript to Clarence, he notified me that he had accepted it for publication. *The Lighthouse Keeper* was my first published book of poetry, quickly sold out two printings, and was selected by the *Small Press Review* as a "pick-of-the-issue." I was privileged to have five additional collections of poems brought out by Timberline Press and El Grito del Lobo Press (the latter was founded by Clarence after he discontinued Timberline Press): *Stark Beauty* (a finalist for both the Poets' Prize/Nicholas Roerich Museum and the Spur Award/Western Writers of America and first runner-up for the Western Heritage Wrangler Award/National Cowboy & Western Heritage Museum); *The Fraternity of Oblivion; The Red Candlelit Darkness* (a Spur Award Finalist); *The Lobsterman's Dream: Poems of the Coast of Maine;* and *Wolves*. All six books were handset letterpress editions featuring original illustrations by Clarence (a serigraph, linocuts and woodcuts).

During the publication of the six books, from 2000 through 2014, Clarence and I became good friends. In April 2011, my wife and I retired to Alpine in far West Texas (I was born and reared in West Texas and resided there until 1967 when I moved to Houston). I knew that Clarence had a far West Texas connection, as he had attended Sul Ross State University in Alpine where he earned his bachelor's degree. Additionally, on three occasions, I was privileged to visit Clarence at his nine-acre woods in Fulton, Missouri.

In early 2013, I proposed to Clarence that he and I engage in a correspondence in poetry which would give us an opportunity to compare and contrast our two quite different environments: the green woods of Missouri vs the high desert of far West Texas. Each of us had composed a large amount of poetry inspired by the natural world, and I thought we would enjoy exploring anew, in poetry, the flora and fauna of our respective home environments of central Missouri and far West Texas. Clarence immediately "got on board" with the idea, and for the next several months (encompassing almost an entire year) we composed the poems of *Wolf Tree and Agave.*

-Larry D. Thomas

Although I was born and raised in Texas, I have lived the latter half of my life in Missouri. Indeed, one's childhood and youthful experiences shape who he is, so I am by gut-instinct a Texan. But for the past five decades, I have been becoming a Missourian. I am talking about place, about familiarity with the natural world around me, about finding the rhythm of the seasons.

I grew up in Bexar County (San Antonio), and although it can be sultry in the summer, it cannot hold a steamy wet blanket to Callaway County, Missouri, where I now live. Those hazy days of August I remember among the mesquite and huisache pale compared to the breezeless and breathless periods in the richness of vegetation here along the Missouri River. I have come to appreciate the differences between my childhood expectations and the natural world that Missouri still presents me. For example, until only the last decade or so, Missouri substituted the groundhog for the armadillo in my catalog of burrowing animals. Now, however, armadillos waddle down my driveway, becoming as comfortable in Missouri skin as I have.

Thus, when Larry Thomas suggested our poetic correspondence in 2013, I welcomed the chance to explore my Missouri by reflecting on Larry's Far West Texas—my Missouri wolf tree in response to his Chihuahuan Desert agave. By the way, for those unfamiliar with the term, a wolf tree is one that has grown in the open, allowing it to branch out horizontally as much as vertically. Wolf trees are difficult, sometimes impossible, to split for fence rails because of the many knots from all the branching.

I also welcomed the chance to enjoy this project with a poet who had become a good friend. We had grown from acquaintances, to poet-publisher, and then to good friends, and Larry and Lisa had been strong support in 2012 when my wife of forty-five years, love of nearly fifty died. I had set out on a quest, based on Patricia's and my mutual vow, to scatter her ashes on the spots that were of special meaning to our life together. The Thomases were with me in Albuquerque when I sprinkled the first vial of ashes in the courtyard of our first apartment, and they were with me when I scattered another handful in Morris Park, Fairmont, WV.

We carried on the poetic experiment for nearly a year. His poem of the windswept song on the Chihuahuan Desert leads to mine about the breath of woodland here on the moraine. My poem about the delicate petals of forest spring blooms is answered by his account of an old man hiking among the hills and rocks near Alpine as winter turns to spring. Poems about geology lead to poems about eccentric characters to poems about the flora and fauna to poems about daily activities. In this exchange, I discovered that like the armadillo I've become habituated to the Missouri woods but still have Southwestern roots; they run parallel and perhaps sometimes even meander into knots.

-Clarence J. Wolfshohl

for Lisa P. Thomas and in memory of Patricia Wolfshohl, our loving wives, soul mates, and friends without whom this correspondence in verse would not exist

"Sir, more than kisses,
letters mingle souls;
For, thus friends absent speak."

— John Donne

On Stationery of Light

I can't remember the last time
I penned a letter to a friend, in cursive,
but I would never have thought
that my next correspondence
would be this: printed with the pressing
of square, black keys on stationery
of light. But here it is, long after
the passing of much too many years.

I've lived in the Great Chihuahuan Desert
for two and one-half years now, perusing
a sky so blue, so vast, and so clean,
even of a wisp or two of clouds,
I find myself probing its depths
as one would a tome of philosophy.

The wind, though, in its myriad forms
often preempts the sky as my preferred
subject of inquiry: wafting, soughing,
and howling like a crazed prophet
long devoid the encumbrances of flesh,
so saturate with sun, moon, starlight,
and the desultory triad of death,
the buzz of flies, and history, he can't stop
the unremitting oozing of his prophecies.

-Larry

Due Cultivation

For me, too, the cursive note
recedes into the silence of the past,
so I'll resort to these keys
to unlock words, often
with more letters than true
orthography demands, the slough
of heavy and stiff fingers.

I key this note from the moraine
shoved and carried to this Missouri edge
from Canadian or Arctic earth
millennia ago. Up the shoreline
of a nearby lake is a perfectly round
stone, some three feet across,
scraped from Minnesota rock,
tumbled smooth and round
on its journey down
the slope of the continent.
It is in a clearing of hickory and oak,
the woods so dense that, but
in winter, you cannot see more
than a moment's walk into their heart.
And this density, this darkness,
is what one must comprehend
in the woods. It is the soil, the clay
so thick a potter dreams, good or bad,
its turning. It is the sky, the dark

silhouetted filigree of leaf and limb
that obscures the blue. It is the breath,
the huff and murmur of wind-inspired crowns,
each tree –sassafras or oak—
speaking its own ancient tongue.

And here on my nine acres
among rolling hills, shallow ponds,
and woodland, a few miles from the Missouri,
the wet mark of the glacier's end,
in these past thirty years I have
tended my garden as old Candide
advised, sometimes with yield,
sometimes without, but always, I hope,
with due cultivation.

May your mad prophet hear the sweet
soughing of my oaks.

                              -Clarence

An Imperceptible Blip

I have been musing
your "silence of the past"
the last few mornings
as I sip my daily coffee
on my balcony. The mountains
to the north, clearly in view
for over forty miles,
are thirty-five million
years old, making
even our millennium
an imperceptible blip
on the black, immeasurable
radar screen of time.

I ponder our fast-forwarded
lives charted for a while
by the brilliantly hued
risings and settings of the sun,
ephemeral as the damaged
legs of a desert millipede,
much too evanescent
for the silliness of war
or the feckless trinity
of dogma, hate, revenge.

-Larry

Tenuous as a Late Autumn Leaf

Cumbrous reflections, indeed, the pace
of any true reflections. But here we are,
my friend, between the eternity
of our geology and the moment
of our biology. We may crave to create
monuments of unaging intellect that rival
the mountains for longevity
and intensity, but we swim in mackerel-
crowded seas. So each of us has a moment
as tenuous as a late autumn leaf.

My granddaughter's elementary school
Veterans Day salute—children's faces alight.
Wide eyes that could see infinity
look out to their parents, grandparents,
teachers expectantly and sing of war
past, present, future; flag that waves
over carnage; and heroes named
in history books. They believe as they
believe seven times seven is forty-nine
with faith that all mathematics
are the same. They close
with the military songs from "off we go
into the wild blue yonder" to
"those caissons keep rolling along."

                              -Clarence

Hooked

Your "swim in mackerel-crowded seas"
brings to mind Balmorhea forty-five miles
to our north, our area's sole desert oasis.
The lake there, fed with the cold, clear water
of San Solomon Springs, is stocked

with bass, crappie, sun perch, and channel cat
Dad, Sam and I fished for the rare weekends
Mom was able to lure Dad from the round-
the-clock clutches of his Mobil service station.
So seldom were the three of us together,

conversation was clipped, difficult
as extricating hooks from the mouths
of caught fish. Mom always stayed ashore
as we fished, sitting for hours on a boulder
and fixing her gaze on the backdrop of purple

Davis Mountains. Her squinted eyes, set against
her Scotch-Irish-bone-white-china skin, glinted
like shards of dark chocolate. She stubbornly
kept her thoughts private, abject and uninviting
as the cool, crackling onionskin of Exodus.

-Larry

A Burl on Oaken Boughs

This is the season of undressing,
despite the turkeys and trimmings
we weave our ways through as days
grow shorter and lights glare brighter.

This is the season of the falling leaf,
the dropping of the skirt of the forest,
and the strewing of its floor
with leaves, and the plying of rakes.

As I pull and push leaves into piles,
trying to decipher the mystery they claimed
a few weeks ago, the darkness they created,
I think of your memories of your father

at Balmorhea, and I remember mine
in my grip on the rake handle, his hands
wrapped around tools or bottles he fed
into a machine for twenty-five years.

Gnarled like roots prizing for veins
of dirt in granite ground, his hands
raked among the leaves of life,
each knuckle a burl on oaken boughs.

The child is father of the man,
says Wordsworth. Our fathers
were the men to our boys,
our branches from which we launched.

-Clarence

The Straw Hat

In the fifties, when Dad
operated his Mobil station
in Midland, the whole world
swirled in a cloud of red dust.
Elsewhere, they called it

"The Filthy Fifties." Among
the most indelible of my childhood
memories are the times I extended
my arms to their limits and couldn't
see my open hands, for the dust.

Sam and I thought it normal,
beautiful even, the way it clotted
our mouths with grit and tried
to crowbar our eyes, ears,
and handkerchief-covered noses.

Once, when we went to Balmorhea,
the red wind lifted Dad's straw hat
from his head and hurled it, frisbee-
like, through the car's open window
right into the canal we crossed

to get to Balmorhea Lake. Dad,
Sam and I chased it for blocks
as it bobbed in the fresh, cold water

of San Solomon Springs. When,
gasping for breath, Dad hooked it

with a fallen branch, he shook it
somewhat free of water
and wore it dripping to the lake,
its wetness short-lived, rarefied
as respite from his Mobil driveway.

-Larry

Eventually

Your father's hat blowing
along the canal at Balmorhea
brings to mind other things
outside our grasp—the career
of sheets of corrugated iron flung
by hurricane winds like cards flicked
by a desperate man toward the trash can
in a dead-end street motel,
or the careening of my neighbor's car
on ice down a curving slope, the driver
resigned to freefall into bare trees
stair-stepped down the steep embankment.
Will they stop him?

The car gains momentum,
a ton of metal skidding
sideways, then swaying
straight, and then shifting
into a 45° angle to the roadway.
The driver's grip cannot
be pried loose. He thinks
to turn off the radio,
Wagner's *Ride . . .*,
which he hasn't liked
since *Apocalypse Now,*
but his hands won't let him.

He remembers his insurance
agent's name but frets
he doesn't know
a tow truck driver.

The trees look farther
from the road in their
winter nakedness. Again,
as the car's driver-side wheel
leaves the roadway and flings
shaved ice from its treads,
he thinks, Will they stop him?
And the other wheels
forget the road, the car
airborne for a moment.
Will they stop him?

-Clarence

Winter Nakedness

During our recent ice storm,
the nights were luminous hells
of bitter cold. Hancock Hill,
when the wind blew, seemed to groan

beneath a three-inch glaze of ice.
Across the hill, secured inside the local
red rock exterior of the Museum
of the Big Bend, loomed the works

of the Remington exhibit, hailed
as the most important *art event*
in the museum's history. Among
the drawings and bronzes of the master,

hung his last painting, untitled,
unofficially referenced as *The Cigarette*
or *Around the Campfire*. Four cowhands,
two of whom are clutching cigarettes,

are hunkered around the fire
beneath a night sky pocked with stars
glowing like the tips of sucked smokes.
The night, as in the other masterworks

for which the artist will be remembered,
is the dominant subject. To the night,
Remington sacrificed the hardest decade
of his life: just to get its color right.

-Larry

Encased

It's the week between Christmas and New Year,
that encased time of the rule of Janus trapped
at this one moment, looking both fore and aft.

Ice sheathes our woods, everything frozen
inside the creak of its casing. The sun is cold,
but it sets the ice afire with gleams.

Is this how the sun shone on Janus after he rode
the current of Styx from the underworld
and collapsed on the icy banks of Eridanus?

It is said, the sun's heat caused the god to sprout
legs, arms, eyes, ears, noses—multiform
blossoms like leaves on a tree.

When our sun warms, our encased world
will shrug off this coating of ice; the carapace
will plunge toward earth, shatter

into fireworks of shine, crescendos
of crackle, and buds will quiver at the tips
of each sprouted limb, within
the hidden pulse of life.

-Clarence

Ice and Fire

pretty much tell our story,
as Frost so eloquently penned
in his piquant, little poem.

One thing I like about living
in far West Texas is the seasons,
all four of them, so unlike the two

in Houston: nine months of summer
and three of spring. The ice here
has cleared, at least for the time being,

and the deer appear to be enjoying
the respite from the cold.
It took the life of a fawn

but the rest of the herd
somehow managed to survive
with nothing but their thickened hide

and the good sense to hunker down
in the dead yellow grasses
for a modicum of momentary

warmth. It's strange how the ice,
so blue with cold and unforgiving,
burns like the flame of a blowtorch.

-Larry

Blue Jays in the Snow

You know where I'm sitting
on this sub-zero, ankle-deep
snowy day. We sat here,
a more full circle, several years
ago and watched the feeding birds.

I remember your love of the cardinal,
like hearts pumping in the bare limbs
of underbrush and against the cedar,
at the feeders and among the juncos.

A few rubricate the text of seed hulls
today, but jays have top billing. One,
perhaps, trails a scraggly feather,
but they are sleek even in their plumps

of blue against the cold. They thrive
in the freeze like young athletes
who play just to feel their bodies
gulp in winter and release a raucous caw.

                              -Clarence

Puma, Cougar, Panther, Mountain Lion

Hancock Hill, on one of whose
northern flanks our house rests,
is not one but several hills
bunched together and separated
by arroyos choked with yucca,
cholla, prickly pear, and whitebrush.

Yesterday, two hikers emerged
from the arroyo near the dumpsters
beside our street, their eyes still wide
from their sighting of two fresh
mule deer kills a half-mile or so
from our house. Local naturalists,

they could tell by the way
the carcasses were ravaged
the kills were the work of a lion.
As they drove away, I pondered
the countless nights it must,
in hunger, have circled our acre,

inching silently through the darkness
on the pliant black pads of its paws,
the circles of its stealth shrinking
with each soft, deliberate step,
tightening the noose of wilderness
around the dewy-eyed throat of our sleep.

-Larry

On the Way to the Funeral

I saw an eagle rise from the roadway.
Powerful strokes lifted it through the heavy air.
The white of its tail opened a door
beyond the day, for an instance, and wings
enraged the smoldering sun into brilliance.

At the funeral, I saw many old friends
and colleagues: more and more,
that's where I see these people. I had
seen the one we buried only two months
ago, at a gathering honoring friends
who were moving to their daughter's
in Illinois. He looked
healthy and hopeful; now
he's dead. We're all getting there,
to our children's or the grave.

The eagle circled and swooped
around the chapel, sparks emitting
from its ponderous wings striking the flint
of all our aging bodies. We all glistened,
for an instance, crimson and gold
and flew with the eagle.

-Clarence

The Black-tailed Jackrabbit

The eagle you spotted
may have been transporting
your deceased friend's soul
to the spirit realm.
It brings to mind

a similar experience
Lisa and I shared
the day we interred
my oldest brother, Jack's,
cremains in the rich red earth

of Henson Cemetery,
Red Springs, Texas.
Red as the earth of his grave
was the narrow dirt road
we had to drive to get there.

After the simple service,
as we headed down the road
to get back to the highway,
a jackrabbit appeared
as if from nowhere

and sat right in the middle
of the road. As it started
zigzagging ahead of us,

stopping, and zigzagging again,
we followed it for a mile

all the way to the highway
till it vanished in a thicket
of mesquite and prickly pear.
Each of us, independently
of the other, felt Jack's spirit

in that black-tailed rabbit
leading us inexorably
onward through the joy-
and-sorrow thickets
of our lives.

-Larry

Today I Did Some Printing,

that transfer of light and line
from plate to paper.
It was an intaglio
for a quixotic book
that eschewed the line
for the light of stars
and a wolf-howling moon.

Quite different from the woodcuts of your book,
their lines being the light of the paper shining
through
the dark of ink, a negative of the poems whose black
lines
enlighten the blank white page.

But the paradox of intaglio
is some necromancer's trick:
the engraved lines barely seen
on the shining surface of plate,
ink pressed deep into those lines
and the plate surface cleaned
again to a shine; the paper
dampened and then pressed
into those lines with enough force
to smash an errant finger.

And then, the print revealed,
lines as light as the thoughts
of children against the white
of infinity.

--Clarence

The Transfer of Light

The high desert light,
intensified by altitude
and clarity of air,
draws artists like moths
to a ubiquitous flame.

One who listens hard enough
can hear the screams of colors
writhing on their canvasses,
jolting the galleries
with cries of the criminally

insane. The lenses
of stout sunglasses
are either mirrors
or dark as leather patches
fashioned to cover

the sockets of gouged eyes.
This winter morning,
through the steam rising
off my coffee, I watched sunlight
crest an eastern flank

of Hancock Hill; skulk
through yucca, dead grass,
and prickly pear; ease down

our driveway sans a sound;
bleed onto the ceramic tile

of our patio; and crash
through the glass of our door
like a flaming puma
leaving in shambles the silly
steel mesh of its cage.

-Larry

What Is Taken Away

My friend, I think of your cougar aflame
and colors that scream, and then read a line
from Colette that a writer is one who
sits down and puts down everything that comes
to mind, but an author is one who knows
to destroy most of it.

All those screaming colors are hidden
behind the pitch black of the cougar,
the everything that comes to mind. A slit
like the gouge of a chisel into wood
is the gate between the colors and the dark
of everything. What is taken away,
destroyed, lets the light in all its array
of colors form the mountains,
the trees, us. What is taken away
shapes what remains.

-Clarence

In All Its Array of Colors

Often, when I'm seated on our balcony
and gaze out toward the mountains to our north,
I think of Balmorhea Lake forty-five miles
(as the proverbial crow flies) distant.
I wait for the memory I know will visit,
constant as morning coffee with my wife.
Today, it's the ten-pound Largemouth Bass,

a pound for each year of my age at the time,
I muscled ashore while fishing with Dad and Sam.
I thought my rod would break, bowed as it was
with the big fish lodging its body beneath rocks
on the lake bottom, thrashing for its life.
I dug my heels deep into the muddy shoreline,
took a deep breath, and reeled in but an inch of line,

it seemed, every five minutes. Exhausted,
I got it ashore and Dad netted it, so proud of me
it hurt us both. We cleaned, filleted, and fried
the thing for supper. Its smell filled our travel trailer
for days, oozing from our pores like fresh garlic.
Even the aluminum Airstream Dad, Mom, Sam and I
tried to fall asleep in, gleamed in the moonglow,

luminous as the scales of a bass.

                              -Larry

The Piscine Y

Your ten-pound bass
and fish-scale sheen
(in your Airstream)
entranced me in
a fisherman's dream.

This morning at the Y
my vision filled with piscine life
as if we were all in an aquarium
or riding the currents of some
creek, river, or sea.

Walkers rounded the track
like goldfish in a bowl
with nowhere to go
except in circles. Most in slow
but consciously paced stride
kept to the outside
glancing at the walls as if they
were glass, and beyond, a strange dry day.

Among the iron, sharks muscled their weights
with grunts and narrowed-eyed concentration—
the body-builders hard as hammerheads,
studious of their skill as great whites. But loud
as sun-perch leaping into sparkles
on a roaring day.

                              Young women sashayed
among treadmills, rowers, and walkers
adorned like fantails and glowing like neon tetra.
They darted their eyes toward the splash and laugh
of the sharks, but kept within the coral tangle
of exercise machines, shy of the sharks' razor teeth.

And then there were we old clown
fish, going through motions to keep
alive —thinking about the pastries
we'd rather be eating or the loungers
we'd rather be reclining in, and rehearsing
the same old self-deprecating lines
about waking up this fine morning
still breathing or wondering why
the stationary bicycles never get us
to our destinations.

                    -Clarence

To Our Destinations

When we moved out here
to the high desert, almost three
years ago, the first thing
many of our Houston friends asked
was what there was to *do* here.

We had already told them
the town had neither a shopping mall
nor even a Walmart, and that
the nearest commercial airport
was a two-hour drive to our north.

They were shocked, breathless
in the frenzy of their own stir-
craziness. Every time I tried
to address their concern, words
unraveled like smoke in the wind.

I knew they'd never understand
we settled out here for nothing
but Mother Desert; for sundowns
vivid as a set of crushed crayons;
for the deer, blue quail, hummingbirds

and javelina sharing the cenizo-
agave-yucca-mesquite-and-ocotillo-
studded acre of our lot; and finally

for the vibrant social life
teeming in the reaches of our psyches

relishing the priceless gift
of the fresh-aired, clear-skied,
and mild-weathered ubiquity
of an isolation so perfected
its silence is a scream.

-Larry

Watching the Chinese Poet Read

At the poetry reading last night
Qian Yang, unsure of his English,
read his long piece in Chinese.

I could not understand a word,
his melodic voice sweeping away
syllable landmarks as soon as,
like phantoms, they arose.
But his hands and fingers spoke
their own and a familiar dialect.

One moment the index, like a conductor's
baton, bounced to the cadence
of his words. Or two, like the Boy Scouts'
salute, waltzed over passages
in front of his chest. When a stanza raised
its pitch his fist closed on its shadow
to lift it higher. And once
in finale, open palm to his listeners,
his hand brushed his forehead
then cheek like a man might his lover.

All those gestures on the air
and sounds drifting to silence
were like the brush strokes
of Chinese characters, each
a symbol in the mural of his poem.

-Clarence

Drifting to Silence

This morning, while soaking up
some welcome sunlight on the patio
and staring at the ram's skull,
I reminisced your, my, and Lisa's
visit to the frontier fort at Fort Davis

twenty-five miles to our northwest.
We pretty much had the place
to ourselves. We heard the reenacted
bugle calls and noise of troops and horses
blaring out over the parade ground

only to unravel in the howling wind.
What stood out most was the hospital
housing the crude and brutal instruments
of the doctors of the day. We winced
at the staggering number of young men

who died not from wounds inflicted
by Apaches and Comanches
but from the silent, invisible bullets,
spears and arrows of dysentery
and disease. Before leaving,

we walked the rugged trail to what
was supposed to be a graveyard.
We thought we found the old tree
marking the spot of the buried,
but never pinpointed an actual grave.

-Larry

Bok Tower Gardens

I've left the foot of snow,
the freezing chill,
the slip-sliding roads
and sidewalks, the wool-
engulfed movements of February
in Missouri for Florida sun.

We stroll now through blooms
of hibiscus and azalea,
through palmetto and saw palm
green, the sun warm
on the face like a lover's kiss
and a breeze that lifts
wispy hair like that lover's
tender words of greeting.

On the breeze and trilled
through the stands of pine
and live oak, the notes
of the carillon tumble down
the tower walls and Iron Mountain,
this highest point on the peninsula,
shaping this day. Orange groves
stand in rows on lower slopes
like the staff of the concerto
the bells peel to accompany
the vibrato of our souls.

-Clarence

Bells

On the flanks
of "A" Mountain
on the south side of town,

towers a three-level belfry
fashioned of native stone.
It's the eastern of two towers

abutting the sanctuary
of Our Lady of Peace
Catholic Church.

On Sunday mornings,
the sound of the bells
drifts down to the town

like sonorous dust,
swirling about the houses,
seeping through open windows,

gracing everything it touches
with a sheen-like film
of sacred hymns.

-Larry

Beached Ice

Down along the Auxvasse
where it wanders a narrow valley
and is crossed by the heavy haul road,
called that by some of us
still thirty years after it carried
the raw materials for the power plant,
the county not wanting damage
to any paved roads,
ice has piled up.

Great slabs of ice,
eight inches thick
like a concrete highway
after an earthquake,
litter the creek's banks,
pushed there by rushing water
after last week's rain and thaw.

They have gouged out
the shoreline, jumped
the bank and stepped
like a sidewalk toward the lone
farmhouse in the tight bend.
A sycamore leans at a 70° angle,
and the ice casts aside
dogwoods with ease.

-Clarence

Brother

I'm in Abilene, Texas,
visiting my older
and last living brother.
There is no ice here today,
in a literal sense that is,
just sky reddened with dust.

My brother's eyes
jerk inside their sockets
like nervous, chocolate birds.
He fixes them on me
only for seconds at a time,
as if they were his fingertips

sizzling on the handle
of a hot iron skillet.
He clutches the arms of his chair
with the trembling,
knobby fingers of *my* hands.
As I look at him, I see *my* face

twelve years from now,
staring back at me
from a sheet of smooth silver
cold in its coffin of glass.
He chokes as the word *love*
lodges in his throat like a stone.

-Larry

The Bounds of Books

Today I bound books—
which is a curious expression,
for can books be bound?
There is a paradox

in binding books—
the collating into signatures,
the piercing in orderly measure
to sew the signatures into a whole,

the gluing on of cover,
and each step marked
by compacting the parts,
the whole, in a vise

tighter than the shackles
of Prometheus, who groaned
out there on Mount Caucasus,
to disguise the book as a block

of wood. And it is a paradox
that Prometheus was bound
for bringing us fire
while books offer light
each time they are opened,
each time they slip their bounds.

                    -Clarence

Hands

for Clarence

Calloused
from the handles
of the hammers and saws

with which you built
your two-story house,
they move through the air

deft as the acrobatics
of hummingbirds.
They are a palimpsest

redolent with the pages
of a million books.
During their finest hours,

when not pressing keys
into poems of light,
they take tweezers,

pinch and lift type
from a type case,
set it with precision

in a composing stick,
ink it, press it
into sheets of linen

paper, and hang them
to dry into pages
of literature.

-Larry

Spring Blooms

Along the Llano and San Saba,
the bluebonnets bloom
followed soon in their blue glory
by Indian paintbrush's layers of red.

But the verbena is always first,
hugging the earth like spots
of purple moss, the first
signs of spring among the hills.

I remember those colors
when here above the Missouri
I see the delicate petals
of the white spring beauty

streaked with pink and rose,
blushing in their nakedness
in the sun after the ice
of winter has unshackled the loam.

                    -Clarence

As Winter Turns to Spring

it relinquishes, begrudgingly,
its reign of parsimony over the desert.
The grasses are pale yellow,
rasping in the wind like dried cornhusks,

parallel to the stony ground
as prostrate, withered penitents.
At daybreak, as if from nowhere,
a faceless old man appears,

ascending an arroyo of Hancock Hill.
His walking stick clacks
against the rocks as he steps,
steadies himself, and steps again.

Breathing heavily, he lumbers on
like a scabrous pilgrim buffeted
by the wind, seeking the naked
shrine of nothing in particular.

-Larry

Tattoo Palimpsest

Seen on a bare-shouldered damsel at the Y

A few tendrils of what must have been
a delicate swirl of vine and blooms
creep from the ebony edge
of the calavera, the skeleton
of the *día de los muertos* motif
rounded on her shoulder. It is
a *señorita* with mantilla of black lace
and filigree pattern on the face
of her skull. Colors from the previous
tattoo show through the fretwork—
the red of what may have been a rose
glows behind half one eye socket,
the blue of a violet winks from the other.

The black of the new tattoo
darkens her shoulder and arm
like an anger that has eclipsed
the motive for the delicate hues
of primrose and violet that lurk
deep within the señorita's skull.

-Clarence

Stones

When we heard
the cold, clear water
of San Solomon Springs

sluicing through the canal
in the heart of Balmorhea,
we knew the lake was near.

The lakefront was steep,
strewn with boulders.
As Dad, Sam and I fished,

Mom, clad in the iron-rich
red of the boulders,
sat for hours on the shore,

staring at the backdrop
of Davis Mountains, so still
she was indistinguishable

from the stones.
I remember being haunted
by her visage, merging

so seamlessly with the rock,
and how she seemed,
though she would live

thirty more years,
already more memory
than vital, breathing self.

-Larry

What to Call It

Lately, a group of dogs
has marked our neighborhood
as its territory, and I'm struck
that all the terms don't fit them.
That is, a name for them collectively.

"Group" is too generic
for these gangly guys.
They are big dogs, some sort
of Lab mixes that will grow
thick and heavy in a year or so,
the kind that will bowl
you over when they nudge
your leg. But now they are lean
and leggy like boys whose jeans
don't cover their ankles
they are growing so fast
and the parents don't want
to buy new pants till the school year.

"Pack" is a word we may use,
but that makes them sound
predatory. They may be, their prey
being fun, but I met them on our gravel
road one day and could see
at a hundred paces they were not
vicious but more like junior high boys

with a ball and bat headed for
a vacant lot for a get-up game,
bumping into one another and jumping
up to touch low branches on overhanging
trees. They couldn't walk straight
with their tails wagging so fast and hard
to throw them off balance,
so they stumbled in joyous dance
toward me and presented their broad
heads for me to scratch—of course,
jostling one another for favored spot—
and licking my hands with their huge,
lolling, slobbering tongues, their eyes
sparkling the kinship of life.

"Gang" doesn't fit either. They aren't
so organized but are thrown together
by the chance of geography and spare time,
perhaps just glad a toy poodle doesn't live
around here to take command
in little dogs' way of compensation.

They are just a bunch of guys
hanging out, a "guy" of teenage
dogs alive and free
on a brilliant blue Saturday.

                                    -Clarence

Near Midnight

My neighbor said he was headed home
late that night, near midnight.
As soon as his pickup turned the curve

in the road to our subdivision,
ascending a flank of Hancock Hill,
he saw the pack coming straight toward him.

Each coyote froze in the glare of his headlights
and stared as he slammed his brakes
and brought his truck to a dead stop.

He said he and the beasts
faced off for several minutes that night
till in a flash, as one, they bolted,

bleeding into the darkness.
He said he'd never forget
their greenish-gold eyes

glowing like the tips of iron rods
twisted from coals by a blacksmith:
their greenish-gold eyes

glowing in folktales where they strutted
as makers of fateful decisions
and stood proud as founders of human arts.

-Larry

Fishing at Lake of the Ozarks

Voices drift over the water,
phrases of the minutiae of the craft—
temperature, depth of water,
glitter of a novice's cast.

The waves glint and open
holes in the water to let
out the sun that plays
in shimmers under our cap-bills.

The celluloid lights dance
with our gaze and blind
us momentarily in the morning
shush of water and wind

until a fish strikes, pulls
the line taut, the nylon
catching a lightning bolt's
surprise parallel to the water.

I reel in the fish and lift it
into luminescence, unhook
it, and re-bait the barb,
a smear of minnow-shine on my hand.

-Clarence

Smear of Minnow-Shine

For me and my younger brother, Sam,
mastering the skill of baiting hooks
without killing, maiming or hooking
the minnows so loosely they jerked
right off the hook, was the hardest part
of fishing with Dad at Balmorhea.

The minnows were expensive so Dad
insisted we learn quickly or resort
to using the plastic purple worms
which bunched so bulkily on the hooks
the barbed tips lay buried in purple.
Much harder even than that, however,

was learning how to fake Mother
into thinking we'd washed our hands
for dinner. Eating, we had to make sure
the undersides of our fish-stenched fingers
stayed hidden from view, preserving
them for our secret, bedtime ritual

as make-believe gods. Just before
snuffing out our bedside candle,
we'd turn in the candlelight, smeared
with sacred minnow-shine, the trembling
fingers fresh from sphering every star,
planet and comet in wide blue heaven.

-Larry

Turkey Strut

My neighbor stopped by this morning to preen
like he said the turkey in the bed of his pickup
had as the sun cleared the trees an hour ago.

Into the clearing charged with three decoys,
it had paced, those long, deliberate strides
the bird takes like a drum major striking up

his band. It had fanned its tail, the bands
of black and brown piped by thin threads
of white. It had fluffed its feathers, shook

its ten-inch beard, and hummed a gobbling
chorus of his turkey love song to the first
homely decoy. She did not strike his fancy,

so he began to mince his steps toward
the second when his passion was ended
with one shot. My neighbor lifted the carcass

from the pickup bed, clear of the bag
it was wrapped in, and a loose sunray caught the
bronze
in an instant, last turkey strut.

                              -Clarence

Laden with What He Needed

for the shoot, he headed up
a flank of Elephant Mountain.
Nearing the summit, he stopped,
eased his binoculars to his eyes,
and surveyed the distance

for the slightest hint of movement
in the brush. Seeing nothing,
he continued his imperceptible
passage with the beast-like stealth
of his target till he came upon

an ideal spot for camouflage.
His clothing was indistinguishable
from the desert flora around him.
He sat Indian-style hidden within
a copse of scrawny trees, slowing

his pulse and muffling his breath
to the brink of silence. For hours,
he kept his downwind vigil,
modulating even the movement
of his eyelids. Suddenly, toward

a single clack of cloven hoof
against rock, he turned his raptor-
like gaze, snapping what he knew
would be his prize-winning photo
of the unsuspecting Aoudad buck.

-Larry

Groundhog

I saw him, a casualty
on the edge of the pavement,
a humped pelt, a few stiff hairs
lifting with the backwash
of passing cars. Thirty minutes
later he scurried from the corner
of my eye on the hillside
above the walking trail.
On the edge of the rip-rap,
a zipper down the hill's green,
he paused when I paused
to watch him. He turned to face me,
then descended into the stones,
into the green hillside.

-Clarence

Giant Boxes

(concrete works by Donald Judd, Chinati Foundation,
contemporary art museum, Marfa, Texas)

the size of small rooms,
of reinforced concrete,
are laid out on the desert
with the precision

of Egyptian pyramids.
The curator worked late,
into the evening, allowing me
to walk the path beside them.

The boxes were open,
occupied with the lavender
air of dusk, lavender
soon turning to black shadow

cast by a Comanche moon.
The wind, with unfettered
access to the boxes,
came and went as it pleased,

oblivious to my presence
as that of the rasping,
yellow grasses.
By the time I left,

the night had assumed
its residence there,
silent and deadly
as always.

-Larry

Wolf Tree

It stands alone on the last bend
of the road before I'm home.
Its limbs spread fifty feet
from the massive trunk, burled
grotesque from broken limbs,
its crown broad and flat.

Yards away is the wall of the woods;
the wolf oak's millions of siblings
stretch miles toward Missouri
bottomland. They spire upward, limbs
turned skyward toward the sun.
They grow straight, no blemish
of burl nor gnarl of wind.

When I split their wood against winter cold,
the grain is long and my maul cleaves
the logs with ease, but the wolf
turns my ax and maul into toys
that bounce off or get trapped
in its sinews. The wolf howls defiance.

-Clarence

Agave

Its dull green leaves
are thick, fleshy,
tipped with a spike
hard and sharp enough
to puncture bone.
It brooks,
for up to thirty years,

all the sun, wind,
hail, and dust
the desert must muster
to pummel it
back to the rock-
strewn earth
from which it sprouted.

For up to thirty years,
it ekes out its harsh
survival, storing
what little moisture
it can wrench
from the bone-dry
heart of desiccation,

starving of thirst
yet storing,
just to thrust,

thirty grueling feet
into the sky, a single
flowering stalk,
and die.

-Larry

Under the Golden Dragon

For the students at the Missouri School for the Deaf

Above the library flies a golden dragon,
above tables, chairs, computers, books,
our heads at this gathering. It is
a Chinese dragon of golden scales

crafted of corrugated cardboard
and of blazing red wings
like flames across the cosmos,
a comet across the dark horizon.

The young poets come forward
with their poems. Their hands
fly with the dragon as they sign
their passions and their dreams.

A girl becomes a mermaid—
fingers, then hands, then arms
swimming through the ocean of her poem.
She dives deep, then rises toward the sun,

catching the glittery gift of its spirit
above with the golden dragon.

-Clarence

We Know We're Well

into spring when
mesquite breaks out
in lacy,
chartreuse leaves;

when ocotillo greens
and the tips
of its branches
thicken with clusters

of buds bursting
into the brilliance
of scarlet flowers.
I see the blotches

of scarlet out there now
through my study
window, blood-red
against the azure

flesh of the sky,
smarting
like fresh,
deep cuts.

                    -Larry

Another Sign of Spring

We and the woods are at odds.
As the temperatures rise,
we begin to disrobe.
First, our parkas, our woolen scarves,
knit hats, the layers of shirts,
long pants, down to shorts
and t-shirts. All winter long,

the trees have stood bare limbed,
leaves shed in piles around their feet.
But now, they begin to weave
new wear. A modesty beyond
their snowbound stoicism. The dogwoods
put on their white linen, the blossoms
so thick my woods glow at night.
Soon will follow the russet buds
of the oak casting a pink haze; then
leaves will unfold like the garments
of morning dressers, who feel
the freshness against their limbs.

-Clarence

Rough Stock

(collegiate rodeo, Sul Ross State University)

The rank bull knows
he owns the pasture,
moving so slowly
one would think
it took his entire strength
to lift a single hoof
or swat a horse fly
with his tail.
Come crunch time,

a strap cinched tight
around his flank,
he'll bolt, when the chute
opens, four feet up
into the air,
twist like a cracked whip,
crash his ton of muscle
to the dirt
on his two front hooves,

fling the rider
to a breathless heap
of embarrassment,
and drive a horn
through his vest
deep into the shattered

cage of his ribs,
all in the space
of four seconds.

-Larry

Breathless Heap

A bull that so explodes
its defiance of inertia bucks
and twists me back decades
to my springtime in those Davis Mountains
and Rodeo Week at Sul Ross.

Those riders of bulls and broncs
spurred on by heritage, dare, or drink
were not the only ones to end
their rides in breathless heaps.

Others rode the long-neck steeds
or bull-dogged 100-proof exhilaration
out in pastures, or in the few motels strung
along US 90, or in the cantinas south
of the Southern Pacific tracks. They
hunkered down, tight-fisted, spurs
flaying, and rode until the sky swirled,
stars jumped their traces,
and up was down.

In the morning, they rose from the dust,
slapped off the ocotillo shreds
from their jeans, scraped off
the prickly pear that danced
on their tongues, and some embarrassed,
some not, searched for another rodeo fling.

                              -Clarence

The Rodeo

(far West Texas)

out here is revered
as an institution
sacred as church,
school, or country.
After all, Alpine's motto

is "Home of the Last
Frontier," but just
because it's the last
certainly doesn't mean
it'll die anytime soon.

Everything enshrines
the glorious West:
the Big Bend Ranch
and Sul Ross State
University Rodeos;

Big Bend Saddlery
and its undisputed reputation
as the top Western tack store
in the world; and Spradley
Custom Hats fashioned

of 100% beaver, so
executed with perfection
even the precise phrenology
of the buyer's head
is felt into the measurement.

-Larry

The Island of Fabled Morels

On an island in the Missouri
just downstream from Jeff City
is a bonanza of morels.
My neighbor told me a workmate
told him, but added the mate
would not tell which island.
Morel hunters are like that,
will not divulge the location
of their hunting grounds,
where the mushrooms gather
in hordes to fill a hunter's pail.

At the Morel & Microbrew Festival
in Fulton, the brew held out all day,
but the morels were gone in an hour.
Harvest wasn't bountiful this spring.
But more than once, as I strolled
among the stands of draft spigots
and deep fryers, I heard whiffs
of conversations about an island
in the Missouri just downstream
from Jeff City.

-Clarence

Grasses

What forest we have
in the Great Chihuahuan Desert
is essentially grasses.
In times of drought
or cold weather, they appear

dead as straw, lying prostrate
on the rocky ground, rustling
in the wind like winter cornstalks.
With but the slightest moisture,
they begin to green again

at their bases, setting out
on their voyages to former
prominence. At night, glinting
the light of a Comanche moon,
they collect the very essences

of Mother Desert: needlelike
slivers of javelina hooves; loose
fur finessed from the paws
of pumas; musk from the oily
passage of diamondbacks;

and the thin, waxen residue
left by the labored breathing
of monogamous gray vixens
birthing, holy with moonglow,
a chorus of mewling kits.

-Larry

Oak Pollen

The catkins hang like worms
in clumps waiting the wind
to ejaculate their golden grains
into a haze of spring air.

The powder fuzzes the light
like dust motes in a sun ray.
For miles the pollen rides
breezes before falling

into female's sticky vessel
to engender an acorn.
All that doesn't fills
window sills and spreads

across windshields so fingers
can wipe "wash me"
onto the golden slate.
With every motion, it swirls

in pirouette up nostrils
to be cast out in explosive
sneeze or to be washed
from eyes in tears of grit.

All that promise of life
we, the allergic, swim
amidst with clogged sinus
wishing we were dead.

-Clarence

Sotol

It stands erect
on the rocky slope
of an arroyo

like a squinty-eyed sentinel
guarding his stubbornness
of survival.

An evergreen rosette,
its tapered, spine-clad leaves
were woven by Native peoples

into mats and baskets.
It stands erect,
this obstinate master

of the art of parsimony,
its grand heart so valued
by the Natives

they baked it in an earth
oven, pounded it into thin
patties, sun-dried them,

and, ofttimes with them
and them alone, if
they were lucky,

eked out the two
brutal decades
of their lives.

-Larry

Shagbark Hickory

Like ragged mendicants
they stand in tatters, bark
shredded and foot littered
with grey shards and nut husks.

These five clustered here
are old and their bark
hangs like the beards
of unkempt holy men.

But they do not beg. They give
the sweet hickory nuts
Indians pounded and steeped
in boiling water to make

a sweet milk used to cook
corncakes and hominy.
Squirrels, bear, fox, turkey, bobwhites
graze the mast, the hickory's

erratic bounty a time of feast
for man, beast, and bird.
The Algonquians gave
us the word "hickory,"

and used its wood to fashion
their bows. We still use that wood:
its hard, tough, long grain good
for ax handles, ploughs, and baseball bats.

                    -Clarence

Terlingua Ghost Town

Today, I rode with a friend
down to Terlingua, one of the few
places left in the country
where one may live anonymously,
secludedly off-the-grid. Ever
unincorporated, it has haunted me

since I first visited it as a child.
The mouths of the old mine shafts
are black, spewing bats at dusk,
wooing men like the jasmine-
scented chanting of Sirens.
The locals speak of the foolhardy

who, succumbing to the urge
to descend, lose their footing,
tumble down the rough,
cold walls of cinnabar,
and crumple like puppets
beneath slackened strings.

From their benches on "The Porch"
of the Terlingua Trading Company,
the locals whisper, facing east,
growing silent as the darkness
nibbling the Chisos, rubbling
the crayons of sundown to dust.

-Larry

O, Pioneer: Our House

Our house was the first frame home
on our twist of a road in these woods.
Four log houses started this community
on Red Bud, spelled as two words
by the old Dutchman who made
the first road sign of cedar's red heart.
Not logs hewn from the miles of white oak
that surround us, but from kits
with each log numbered like a giant
doll house, some assembly required.
Two other frames started a month or two
afterwards, but this one—ours—was the pioneer.

None of the log houses are occupied
by the original families—death, divorce, age.
We built a frame house because I knew how
after many summers turning brown
as a berry on the concrete-slab prairies
of construction boom San Antonio.
So Patricia sighted walls and plumbed
corners while I used pulleys and ropes
and the surrounding trees to muscle
two-by skeletons straight and true.
All three of the frame houses are still occupied
by the original families although smaller—
death, divorce, age.

I awoke this morning dreaming
of our pioneer days building
this house, this community,
our white smiles all over
our brown berry faces,
and Patricia's eye squinting
along a top plate that had no ending.

-Clarence

Ursus Americanus

Word is the black bear
returned to the Big Bend
sometime in the 1980s,

having ambled hundreds of miles
from the Sierra Madre Oriental
of Mexico to the Chisos Basin.

The three-hundred-pound sow
first appeared as a dark shadow
moving through underbrush.

In no time she blocked The Window
Trail I was hiking that late October
morning, freezing but a few feet

in front of me. I had already frozen,
suppressing fear because I knew
she would smell it. I slowed

my breath and pulse almost
to the point of passing out.
She turned her great head

slowly toward me, and our eyes met.
Each of her three-inch claws
retracted in the black leather pads

of her paws was a relic
of all the wilds of Mexico.
Her belly stretched taut

with sotol hearts and juniper berries,
she wasn't a threat as long as
I kept my fearless countenance

and stared her down sans blinking,
willing myself, brain,
heart, muscle, bone, and soul,

to the lacquered,
inanimate hickory
of my walking stick.

                              -Larry

The Ghosts of Toledo

(Toledo, Callaway County, Missouri)

I walked down the shaded slope
across Craighead Branch east
into Toledo, to the crossroads
where two gravel and two paved roads
meet, charting how the county
judges our neck of the woods.

A few rock foundations are scattered
through the woods, filled with brush
or third growth oaks. They crumble
around the roots, whisper chorus
to the squawks of jays.

The old school house releases birds
from windows and roof holes,
where legend says Jesse James
hid and taught among veteran
guerillas in the village of two hundred.

Only the old Unity Church
with its churchyard of stones
and decaying crosses dating back
to the 1840s still stands.
Even a house across from the church
on the crossroads, built
after I first walked these woods,
now composts with those older ghosts.

At night owls moan among the oaks
and fox scream like women in pain
down the hollows in mating season.
As I walk home, the sun sinks behind
far ridges, the darkening shades
of purple before me joining the hum.

-Clarence

Hereford Bull

For several mornings in a row,
he has stood against the barbed wire fence
along the road to our subdivision,
staring at the pasture across the road.

I wonder what he's thinking,
if bulls think at all. Does he miss
the company of his kind? Or is he
simply basking in a sun older

than his primitive progenitors in England,
striking his red coat into fire?
Perhaps he's only reveling in his instincts:
chewing his cud; swatting flies

with his bushy, white-tipped tail;
entranced by the throbbing bass drum
of his heart; flaring thick nostrils
for the scent of a cow in heat.

                                        -Larry

They Wear It Well

5th Grade Graduation at Woerner School

The girls are dressed
in their party best
newly bought for today
or Christmas or Easter dresses
that sheen with metallic polish
or that flounce in diaphanous
sympathy with the spring morning.

The boys have combed
their hair, tucked in shirt-
tails. Some with polished
shoes, some with erratically-
knotted ties. A few wear
suits purchased for special
occasions—funerals
or weddings—last summer
or even at Christmas, but now
with sleeves too short
and pants legs above ankles.

Even so, the boys are nearly a head
shorter than the girls, those young
ladies who still stomp impatient strides
down the hall, but today take demur
steps across the stage.

                              -Clarence

The Vaquero

In the late afternoon shadows, after
I had swilled a couple of Shiner Bocks
in the outdoor part of Harry's Tinaja,
he sat across from me at a table

darkened with the thick, waxen residue
of years of spilled beers. He swilled
a Carta Blanca. His palm straw hat
was even darker than the table, blackened

with decades of sweat, his boots so worn
I couldn't figure how they stayed on his feet.
When I spoke he nodded, slightly smiled,
but never said a word. I thought he was mute.

We alternated buying rounds of beer,
mine Shiner Bock, his Carta Blanca.
It was obvious he worked livestock, reeking
as he did of the sweat and slobber of horses.

His spurs, dark with tarnish, jangled
as he made his way to the men's room
and soon returned for another beer.
He walked with a hobbling gait,

as if stepping down from a curb. As night fell,
when my turn came to buy a round, he rose,
leaned toward me, and rasped, "You know,
Señor. We were the first cowboys." Then left.

-Larry

The Sign-Painter

He's one of those cantankerous Missourians,
like the old man down at Jerome
with his Trail of Tears memorial,
said voices told him to build it,
voices of Cherokee who crossed
that way to Oklahoma, so he did.
Concrete statues, wishing wells,
A white buffalo. Jesse Howard's shrine
was of words painted on signs.

No voices, just his begrudged self.
The town now calls the hill
Sign-Painter. He called it
Sorehead Hill. Covered it
with signs and wonderers—
windmills and crude wooden planes,
spinning and catching uplifts
among outlaw words.

The black and red words
of Biblical import, of outraged
justice, of municipal resistance.
The pointed fingers punctuating
the text like the thump
of hallelujah.

-Clarence

The Desert Heat

is upon us,
scorching our eyes
like the dry heat-
blast of a quickly
opened oven.

How even the vultures
survive it
is a mystery,
their dark swirls
filling the sky

like black dust devils.
The deer dig scrapes
beneath mesquite,
lying down
in clouds of dust.

The yuccas
thrust their sword-
shaped leaves
into the sky,
defiant

as Beethoven
on his death bed,
challenging God
with his raised,
trembling fists.

-Larry

Chicory Blues

The chicory sings the blues
along the roadway, but it's no
low-down blues, no head-sunk,
tear-dropping blues. It's pick-me-up
blues like a morning cup of joe,
a tonic for what ails you,
a hard-thumping boogie
infusion of your feet, a soul-
piercing, cosmos-joining
dance of the blue flower.

The chicory sings today
a midsummer day's song
of imagination ripe,
upper and lower worlds
mingled, lovers drugged
on kisses, on petal dewdrops
in the eyes, on flowers
that drain the sky's blue
into their veins and seep
it out along the roadway
from azure petals.

                        -Clarence

Gloria

When queried about her heritage,
she flashes a broad smile and says
both of her parents were Mexican.
In her mid-eighties, she still works

part-time when jobs are available:
cleaning houses and the rooms
of local motels; washing and ironing
clothes; and helping her great-grandson

with yard work. She has lived
her entire life in a small adobe house
at the base of "A" Mountain. During
the hot months of May, June, and July,

she opens her screened windows
and doors, with but a ceiling fan
to keep the air moving, only during
the hottest part of the day. She learned

early on that the best friends of her life
would number only three: Wind,
Sun, and Dust; that these she could
always count on. Evenings, after

Sun retires for the night and Dust
settles gently on her roof, yuccas,
ocotillos and agaves like the laying
on of hands, she anticipates the certain

arrival of Wind, swirling her rustling
skirt, whispering non-stop, till Gloria
falls soundly asleep, the mellifluous,
innocuous murmurs of her gossip.

-Larry

Armadillos and Groundhogs

My friend from Boone County says
he has never seen a live one,
and I haven't in Missouri, except
for one ambling along I-44 near Joplin
just across the Oklahoma line.
North of the Missouri, I see
only the dead, usually at bridge
abutments as if they'd paid no heed
to Sign painter Jesse's warning,
on the curviest road as it enters
the narrowest bridge, to get right
with Jesus. Or maybe they had.

In my youth in Texas, I also saw
many cracked shell armadillos
on the roads, but as many or more
of the live grubbing in gardens
and orchards or rambling down
sunbaked right-of-ways. Here
they are still rare, the local rooting
species being groundhogs. I see
them, the color of rich loam,
live and dead on the roads or berms.

I expect to see whistle pigs
on my way to town; they
are comfortable inhabitants

of my inner landscape, but armadillos
appear at awkward angles,
cracked and inert, like one
of the carcasses that never
made it across the bridge.

                              -Clarence

Larry D. Thomas, a member of the Texas Institute of Letters and the 2008 Texas Poet Laureate, resides in Las Cruces, New Mexico. He has published several award-winning and critically acclaimed collections of poetry, including *As If Light Actually Matters: New & Selected Poems* (Texas A&M University Press Consortium 2015) which was selected as a 2015 Writers' League of Texas Book Awards finalist. His *Larry D. Thomas: New and Selected Poems* (TCU Press 2008, Texas Poets Laureate Series) was longlisted for the National Book Award (the 2013 longlist was the first to be announced to the general public). His most recently published collections are *In a Field of Cotton: Mississippi River Delta Poems* (Blue Horse Press 2019) and *Boiling It Down: The*

Electronic Poetry Chapbooks of Larry D. Thomas (Blue Horse Press 2019). Among the journals in which Thomas's poems have appeared are the *Southwest Review, Poet Lore, JAMA: Journal of the American Medical Association, Christian Science Monitor, Callaloo: A Journal of African Diaspora Arts and Letters, Southwestern American Literature, Green Hills Literary Lantern, San Pedro River Review, Arkansas Review: A Journal of Delta Studies, Delta Poetry Review, Valley Voices: A Literary Review* and *Taos Journal of Poetry.* His Web site address is www.larrydthomas.com.

Clarence Wolfshohl, professor emeritus at William Woods University, has been active in the small press as writer and publisher for over fifty years, publishing poetry and non-fiction in many journals, both print and online, including *North Dakota Quarterly, Concho River Review, San Pedro River Review, Agave, Green Hills Literary Lantern, Cape Rock, New Letters, Southwestern American Review, Gasconade Review, Home Planet News, and The Mailer Review.* Among his recent publications are the e-chapbook *Scattering Ashes* (Virtual Artists Collective, 2016), the chapbooks *Holy Toledo* (El Grito del Lobo Press, 2017), *Queries and Wonderments* (El Grito del Lobo Press, 2017), *Armadillos & Groundhogs* (2019), *Scattering Ashes* (El Grito del Lobo, 2025), and his collection *Play-Like* (Alien Buddha Press, 2025). He has been nominated for a Pushcart Prize twice. Wolfshohl lives in the suburbs of Toledo, Missouri, with his two cats.

This project was made possible, in part, by generous support from the Osage Arts Community.

Osage Arts Community provides temporary time, space and support for the creation of new artistic works in a retreat format, serving creative people of all kinds — visual artists, composers, poets, fiction and nonfiction writers. Located on a 152-acre farm in an isolated rural mountainside setting in Central Missouri and bordered by ¾ of a mile of the Gasconade River, OAC provides residencies to those working alone, as well as welcoming collaborative teams, offering living space and workspace in a country environment to emerging and mid-career artists. For more information, visit us at www.osageac.org

Osage Arts Community

www.ingramcontent.com/pod-product-compliance
Lightning Source LLC
Chambersburg PA
CBHW020742130626
46554CB00006B/2112